50 HOMEGROWN RECIPES FROM A
TAIWANESE-AMERICAN FAMILY

NOMS from MOM
THE COOKBOOK

WRITTEN BY NANCY JENG
ILLUSTRATED BY NANCY JENG
PHOTOGRAPHY BY NANCY JENG
RECIPES BY MOM

Orange Cloud Press

For Mom, Dad & Susan
In loving memory of Nai Nai

CONTENTS

Starters & Sides 13

Main Dishes 53

Drinks & Desserts 111

The Larder 137

PREFACE

Not so long ago, my mom would have said that I am the last person she'd expect to write a cookbook about Taiwanese food. There are a few reasons why she would rightfully think this. One, having been born and raised in California, my mom would say that I have a very American perspective on life, food and the world. Two, I'm really not that great of a cook (sucks for you, reading this cookbook!), though I do enjoy it and love learning. Three, it wasn't until fairly recently, in adulthood, that I've genuinely expressed interest in my Taiwanese heritage. This has manifested most prominently in food, but percolates to all aspects of my life.

My husband and I recently had brunch with a friend I've known since childhood. I mentioned I'm working on this cookbook and my husband commented that my friend must be familiar with my mom's cooking, having grown up with me while I was under my parent's roof. But the truth was, she didn't really know about my mom's amazing cooking or the dishes I've now grown to love.

As a young tween growing up in the 90s, I was dead set on acculturating with the world I saw in my favorite magazines, movies, and TV shows. At the time, this meant suppressing the parts of me, my food, and culture that felt 'different'. I wanted the Americanized lunchboxes and dinners that other kids had. As a result, my mom would often cook a separate dinner for me and my sister (think: spaghetti and meat sauce, macaroni and cheese) or I'd begrudgingly eat the Taiwanese dishes she made, usually with a stink face (or Chòu liǎn, as we say in Chinese).

It wasn't until moving away for university, and some sobering family health scares, that I really started to appreciate what I had. And as I matured as an adult (because let's face it, I was a terrible teen), I felt a renewed sense of identity and pride in the Taiwanese heritage I had been running from for so long. I started legitimately craving Chinese home cooking. I became more curious about my mom and my grandma's cooking techniques and recipes. And one fateful summer, when a house renovation gone long brought us back to my family home, I started the Noms From Mom blog.

In many ways, this project is long overdue. But however it came about and however long it took, here we are. I couldn't be more proud now to share this piece of myself, my mom and our family soul through this labor of love. I hope you enjoy it as much as I've loved making it.

Cheers,
Nancy

INTRODUCTION

The best Chinese cooking is not based on recipes, but rather a medley of other factors. Ingredients are driven by what's in season or oftentimes, what's on sale (gotta love a good deal). Instructions are based on feel and taste instead of precise steps. Measurements are scoffed at - you just know when it's right.

So embarking on this journey to capture our family recipes was an endeavor just short of insanity. The process to get here involved many phone calls back home ("what kind of tofu do we use for chive boxes?") and hours spent hovering over mom's shoulders in the kitchen ("what did you just put in that soup?"). Not to mention the many Google translate detours I took, trying to uncover dish names and phonetic translations.

All this to say, there's a few caveats to consider as you navigate this cookbook. Cooking discretion is advised.

THERE'S CHINESE. THERE'S ENGLISH. AND THERE'S JENGLISH.
In this book, you'll find nicknames, Jeng-isms, Chinese names and Americanized translations. Not all dish names are official names and in fact, many dishes didn't even have names (so pardon us if we got a little creative). Even when the words don't translate, we hope that the food will.

BE SCRAPPY WITH YOUR SCRAPS.
In the hundreds of times we've made dumplings, bao and wontons, we have never once gotten the exact right ratio of filling to wrapper. But constraints breed creativity! So extra dumpling dough turns into a pastry dessert and extra meat can make for a tasty stir-fry. They key is to be resourceful, creative and never. waste. food. In fact, many of our favorite recipes were born out of leftover ingredients.

THERE'S MORE THAN ONE WAY TO FOLD A DUMPLING.
This is not an actual saying, but you get the gist. Recently, we discovered that everyone in our family makes lion's head meatballs in a different way (none of which are the 'traditional' way). Similarly, all the recipes in this book should be viewed as suggestive - feel free to make each dish your own.

EAST MEETS WEST

中西合併

Zhōngxī hébìng

STARTERS & SIDES

GREEN ONION PANCAKES

蔥油餅 | Cōng yóubǐng

Serving Size: 4

Green onion pancakes are a staple in our lives – perfect as a side dish for any dinner and, if you throw an egg on it, it's a delicious breakfast as well. This is also a dish that everyone on my mom's side of the family makes in a different way. Despite the different methods, it's unanimous that Nai Nai's pancakes reign supreme. Below is her recipe, along with a photo cameo on the next page.

1/2 cup green onion, chopped

2.5 cups flour

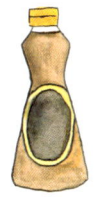

1 tsp sesame oil

1/2 tsp salt

1 cup hot water

1 Mix flour and hot water to form a soft dough. Shape into a ball, cover with a damp cloth, and prove for 45 minutes.

2 On a floured surface, roll the dough out into a large circle. Drizzle sesame oil and spread evenly to cover the dough. Sprinkle salt on the sesame oil, then cover with green onions.

3 Roll the dough up into a long strand. Cut the strand into quarters. You should now be able to see the spirals of green onions where you made your cuts.

4 Pinch and seal the ends so that the spirals and green onions are not showing. Lightly shape into balls and cover with a damp cloth to rest for another 30 minutes.

5 On a floured surface, roll out the four dough balls into a flat pancake shape. You now have your pancakes! You can pan fry them immediately in a skillet or freeze them for later.

6 To pan fry, add some cooking oil to a large flat pan. Cook on each side until browned, a few minutes each.

SMASHED CUCUMBER SALAD
凉拌黄瓜 | Liángbàn huángguā

Serving Size: 4

Watching my Nai Nai make this dish was always a treat. Even at 90 years young, she was a whiz in the kitchen. Give this woman a cleaver and she'd smack the hell out of some cukes like nobody's business.

2-3 small cucumbers (1/2 pound)

1 tbsp rice vinegar

1/2 tsp salt

1 tbsp sugar

1 clove garlic, grated

1/2 red chili pepper

1/2 tsp soy sauce

1 Cut cucumbers into 2-inch chunks, then quarter them OR take the flat side of a knife to it and whack it to give it a good smash. They should break apart into about 4 pieces naturally.

2 Salt the cucumbers and let them sweat for 10-15 minutes. Drain the liquid.

3 Toss in vinegar, soy sauce, sugar, garlic, and red peppers. Let them marinate another 10 minutes before serving.

TOMATO EGG
蕃茄炒蛋 | Fānjiā chǎo dàn

Serving Size: 4

There is no other dish (and one might actually consider this a 'side') that encapsulates my childhood eating memories more than Tomato Egg. Because this dish is so quick and simple, it's become almost as much of a staple as white rice at family meals.

2 tomatoes

1 tbsp cooking oil

4 eggs

3 tbsp water

1 tsp soy sauce

Salt and pepper to taste

1 Heat up some oil in a wok or frying pan, add chopped tomatoes and stir-fry for 2-3 minutes. Add water and cook for another minute. Remove and set aside.

2 Scramble the eggs in the same hot wok, leaving it slightly runny. When the eggs are near ready, add tomatoes back in along with soy sauce.

3 Add salt and pepper to taste. Serve with rice and other dishes as part of a family meal.

SHREDDED TOFU SALAD
凉拌豆腐丝 | Liángbàn dòufu sī

Serving Size: 4

This quick and easy appetizer is a family favorite and one of my Nai Nai's specialties. There are many variations on this dish that exist, but my Nai Nai's was always a very simple, light but flavorful take. We'd often eat these at the beginning of a meal and frequently ordered it at restaurants alongside classic beef noodle soup. It's hard not to think of her when making this dish and I hope she's proud of how we've recreated it.

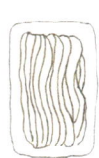
1 8 oz package of tofu strips

1 small carrot, julienned

2 stalks of Chinese celery, julienned

1/4 cup loosely packed cilantro

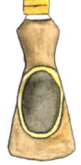
1 tbsp sesame oil

1 tsp salt

1/8 tsp black pepper

1/4 tsp Mama Jeng's chili oil (see recipe)

1. Slice carrots and Chinese celery into thin strips. If using regular celery, one rib should be enough.

2. Bring a pot of salted water to a boil and cook the tofu strips for 3 minutes. While the water is still boiling, use a strainer to blanch the carrots.

3. Remove tofu and carrots from the pot and rinse immediately in cold water.

4. Toss tofu, carrots, celery, and chopped cilantro together with sesame oil, salt, pepper and chili oil. Taste and adjust seasoning as desired.

"CHINESE FRENCH FRIES"
炒洋芋 | Chǎo Yángyù

Serving Size: 4

When we were little, my mom used to name some of her classic dishes after more westernized foods so that my sister and I would be more receptive to them. Of course, this was before I became the worldly, culturally confident individual I am now. Which brings me to Chinese French Fries. What an oddly named dish, right? This side dish or meal accoutrement is so easy to make and as you can imagine, a huge hit with kids. It's a savory julienned potato that goes great with any number of main dishes and I especially enjoy it with tomato egg.

1 Russet potato

Salt, to taste

1 Peel potatoes, then slice them julienne-style into thin, even strips. For this dish, the thinner the better.

2 Heat up oil in a pan, then toss potatoes in. Keep tossing as it cooks and add soy sauce after a minute of cooking. It should sizzle!

3 Salt as needed.

1 tbsp soy sauce

1 tbsp cooking oil

DRY-FRIED GREEN BEANS

乾煸四季豆 | Gān biān sìjì dòu

Serving Size: 4

I remember being shocked to learn that the green bean dish we all know and love from Chinese cooking is actually fried (like, deep-fried). Green beans are supposed to be healthy right?! No wonder these are so addictive and yummy.

1 pound of green beans

1 cup oil for deep frying

1 tsp pickled kohlrabi (optional)

1 tsp dried shrimp (optional)

2-4 cloves garlic, minced

1 tbsp soy sauce

Salt and pepper, to taste

1. [Optional] Soak the pickled kohlrabi and the dried shrimp in a cup of warm water for 15 minutes before starting.

2. Heat up the oil and fry the green beans in batches for a few minutes until it starts to become slightly wrinkled. Remove and place each batch on a paper towel.

3. Drain the oil and but leave a little bit in the pan to cook the rest of the dish. Saute the pickled kohlrabi, dried shrimp and garlic in the oil.

4. Add green beans, soy sauce and salt & pepper to taste. Serve while hot.

KOHLRABI STIR-FRY WITH BEEF & CARROTS

牛肉炒大頭菜 | Niúròu chǎo dàtóucài

Serving Size: 4

Not gonna lie, I'm not sure I knew what kohlrabi even was before this dish. It's a funny-looking vegetable with a funny-sounding name. Kohlrabi is fairly cheap and found in most Asian grocery stores (and in Taiwan, the kohlrabi is huge!), but just one head goes a long way in this dish.

1 head of kohlrabi

1 large carrot

6 oz flank steak

1 tbsp soy sauce

Salt, to taste

1. Peel kohlrabi and carrots and julienne into thin strips.

2. Slice flank steak into thin shoestring-sized pieces. Pro tip: this is easier to do if the beef is frozen first, then slightly thawed.

3. Marinate steak pieces in soy sauce and sesame oil.

4. In a wok or large pan, saute the beef until just cooked through, then add kohlrabi and carrots. Add salt to taste.

TURNIP CAKES
蘿蔔糕 | Luóbo gāo

Serving Size: 12 pieces in a loaf
Turnip cakes are a classic dim sum staple and a favorite in the Jeng family household. When we eat out, we'll usually place a double order of turnip cakes just to make sure there are enough (and because my husband can eat an entire order on his own). This homemade version is great to keep in the freezer to cook up on demand. This recipe is light on salt as it's meant to be served with soy sauce and chili oil.

1 pound of daikon (medium-sized)

1 tbsp dried shrimp

2-3 dried shiitake mushrooms

1 heaping tbsp dried shallots

1 Chinese sausage

2 cups rice flour

1/4 cup corn starch

2 tbsp cooking oil

450g + 600g water, separated

2 tsp salt

1/2 tsp pepper

1 Grease an 8-inch loaf pan. Soak the mushrooms and shrimp in hot water for 15 minutes to rehydrate.

2 Peel and shred the daikon. Optional: leave a few chunky pieces for additional texture.

3 Drain the mushrooms and shrimp and chop into small pieces. Chop sausage into small pieces and set aside.

4 Mix rice flour, corn starch, and 450g water in a large bowl until well blended. Add salt and pepper.

5 Heat oil in a large wok and stir-fry the mushrooms, sausage and shrimp for 2-3 minutes. Then add the shallots and daikon and cook for an additional 3-5 minutes.

6 Pour in the 600g water and bring to a boil for 3 minutes. Turn heat to low, pour the rice flour mixture in, and quickly stir before the mixture coagulates. Turn off the heat and continue to stir quickly until thoroughly mixed.

7 Spoon the mixture into the greased loaf pan. Start boiling water and place loaf pan in a steamer once the water is boiling. Steam for 40 minutes.

8 Cool and store in the freezer or fridge for whenever you're ready to make the dish. To cook, slice into 1/2-inch slices and pan-fry in oil for a few minutes on each side. Serve with soy sauce and chili oil.

EGG DROP SOUP WITH CORN
玉米蛋花湯 | Yùmǐ dàn huā tāng

Serving Size: 4

Most people know this dish as egg drop soup, but in our family, this was always called "corn soup". Adding corn was a twist my mom added to make this dish heartier and yummier. I have fond memories eating this soup on winter nights, when combating a cold or as a nice quick addition to a meal of pot stickers.

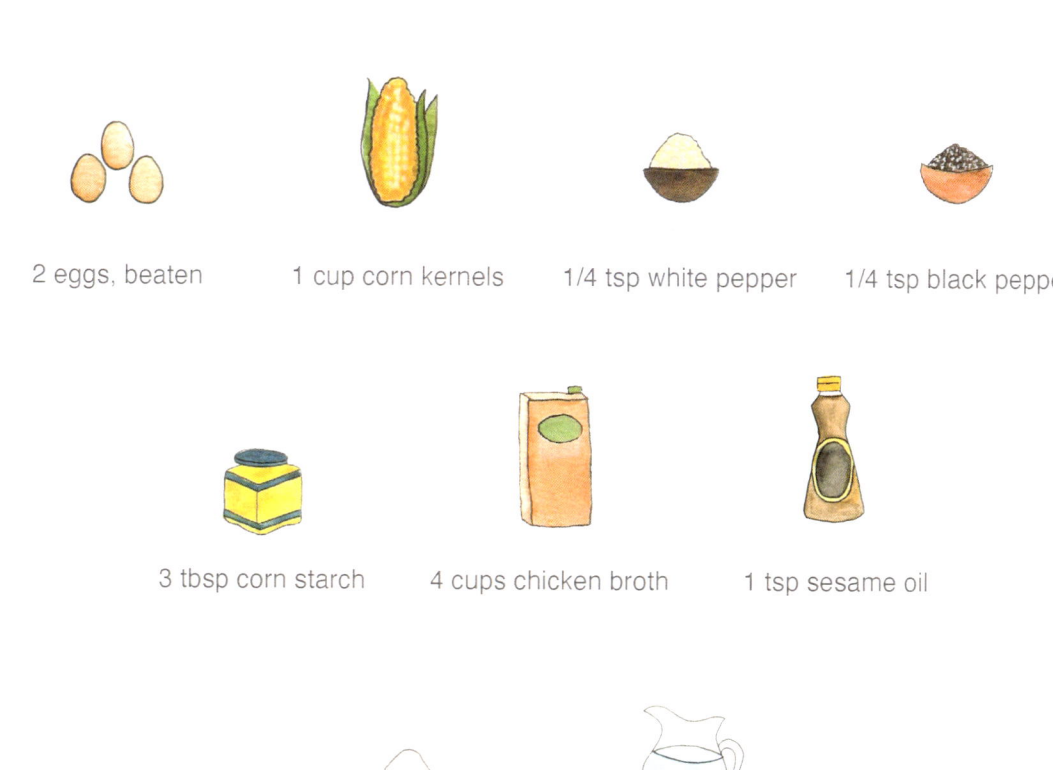

2 eggs, beaten   1 cup corn kernels   1/4 tsp white pepper   1/4 tsp black pepper

3 tbsp corn starch   4 cups chicken broth   1 tsp sesame oil

1/2 tsp salt   1/2 cup water

1. Heat chicken broth, then season with sesame oil, salt, white pepper, black pepper.

2. Mix corn starch and water in a separate bowl, then add into the soup and stir to mix.

3. While stirring the broth, slowly pour in the beaten eggs to create a swirled mixture.

4. Add corn and stir for an additional minute. Season to taste.

LOTUS ROOT STIR-FRY
椒麻醋溜蓮藕 | Jiāo má cù liū lián'ǒu

Serving Size: 4

As someone who is a self-diagnosed trypophobic, it's a little strange that I love lotus roots as much as I do. Not only are they cool-looking, but the crunchy texture is unlike anything else. The following is an easy recipe mom uses for a quick veggie side dish. It takes 15 minutes to make and is a great textural add to any family meal.

1 pound of lotus root

1 red chili pepper, sliced thinly

1 tsp Szechuan peppercorns

1 tbsp soy sauce

1/2 tsp sugar

1/2 tsp salt

2 tsp cooking oil

1/2 tsp vinegar

1. Peel lotus and cut into thin slices. Rinse lotus slices in water to remove starch.

2. Heat cooking oil in wok and roast the peppercorn until browned. Remove the peppercorns from the oil and discard.

3. Add chili, stir for a minute. Then add lotus, soy sauce, sugar, salt. Stir fry for about 5 minutes.

4. Drizzle vinegar, stir briefly, then plate and serve hot.

"POT STICKER" TOFU
鍋塌豆腐 | Guōtiē dòufu

Serving Size: 4

This dish is nicknamed Pot Sticker Tofu because you get that crispy crust from pan-frying like you do with a pot sticker dumpling. But unlike real pot stickers, this dish is veggie-friendly and super, super quick and easy to make.

- 1 16 oz package firm tofu
- Salt & pepper to taste
- 1 egg, beaten
- 1 cup flour
- 2 tbsp cooking oil
- 2 tbsp soy sauce
- 1 tsp sugar
- 1 tsp sesame oil

1 Slice tofu into flat squares, about 1 cm thick. Sprinkle with salt and pepper and marinate for 15 minutes.

2 Heat oil in a fry pan. Drench tofu in egg, then flour, and pan fry for a few minutes on each side until golden brown. Lay on a paper towel as you finish each batch.

3 Mix soy sauce, sugar and sesame oil in the hot pan, then toss tofu in sauce quickly to coat.

4 Plate and garnish with green onions if desired.

STEAMED EGG
蒸蛋 | Zhēng dàn

Serving Size: 4

This may be the dish that we've made the most, ever. It's super simple and we almost always have the ingredients on hand. And yet, despite the hundreds of times we've made steamed eggs, when I called my mom to confirm the ratio of egg to water in this recipe and her response was "no idea". What can you do? Here goes.

3 eggs

1/4 tsp salt

1-1/2 cup water

Drizzle of soy sauce

Drizzle of sesame oil

1. Beat eggs with water and salt in a steamer-safe bowl. Optional: beat in a separate bowl and pour into steamer-safe bowl through a sieve to get out the air bubbles.

2. Bring a pot of water to a boil in a steamer, then place egg dish inside and steam for 15 minutes until set but still jiggly. *Note: Steam times may vary depending on the bowl - thicker bowls take longer to cook.*

3. Drizzle sesame oil and soy sauce over the top. Serve hot with rice and other dishes.

DRY BEAN CURD WITH SHREDDED PORK

香乾肉絲 | Xiāngqián ròu sī

Serving Size: 4

There are many names for this dish - five spice tofu with pork, dried pork shreds - none of which sound particularly appetizing. We often serve this alongside an egg dish (steamed egg, tomato egg), green veggies, Chinese French fries and rice. You can also sub in beef or chicken instead of pork (which is actually sliced, not shredded, despite the name).

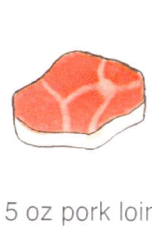
5 oz pork loin

10 oz dry bean curd

1 red chili pepper

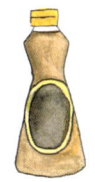
1 tsp sesame oil

1/2 tsp salt

1/4 tsp pepper

1 tbsp soy sauce

1 tbsp cooking oil

1. Slice the pork, tofu and chili pepper into long thin strips. Pro tip: freeze the pork in advance and slightly thaw before slicing to get precise, thin cuts.

2. Marinate the pork in sesame oil, salt and pepper for 5 minutes.

3. In a wok or pan, heat cooking oil on medium-high and cook the pork until browned.

4. Toss in the sliced tofu and chili pepper and cook for an additional 2 minutes.

5. Add soy sauce and salt and pepper to taste.

SHRIMP LETTUCE CUPS
生菜蝦鬆 | Shēngcài xiā sōng

Serving Size: 8 lettuce cups

This is inspired by a well-known dish at a long-standing Bay Area Chinese restaurant, Chef Chu's, in Los Altos. This is a lighter take on it with different options for ingredients depending on what's on hand.

8 lettuce leaves (iceberg or butter) | 1 pound of shrimp | 2 tbsp water chestnuts, chopped (or bamboo shoots) | 1 oz Chinese donuts, toasted and crushed (alt: fried wonton skins)

   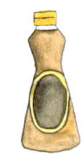

1/4 cup cooked peas or edamame beans | 1/4 cup carrots, diced | 2 tsp cooking wine | 1/2 tsp sesame oil

1/2 tsp salt | 1/4 tsp white pepper | 2 tbsp cooking oil

1 Peel and de-vein the shrimp, and dry thoroughly with a paper towel. Chop the shrimp into pea-sized pieces, then marinate with the cooking wine, white pepper, salt, sesame oil for 10 minutes.

2 Wash and dry lettuce leaves. Prepare and chop all the other ingredients.

3 Heat up 1 tbsp oil in a wok and stir-fry shrimp until pink. Remove and set aside.

4 Cook the peas (or edamame), carrots, and water chestnuts (or bamboo) for 2 minutes on medium-high heat.

5 Add shrimp back in and toss in fried wonton skins or Chinese donuts. Serve with lettuce leaves while warm.

SPICY BASIL EGGPLANT

紅燒茄子 | Hóngshāo qiézi

Serving Size: 2

According to mom, the defining feature of this recipe is how the purple color of the eggplant remains preserved throughout cooking. To do this, you need a large flat pan to cook the eggplant skin side up - it's all for the aesthetics, clearly! Besides the beautiful purple color, this dish is garlicky goodness.

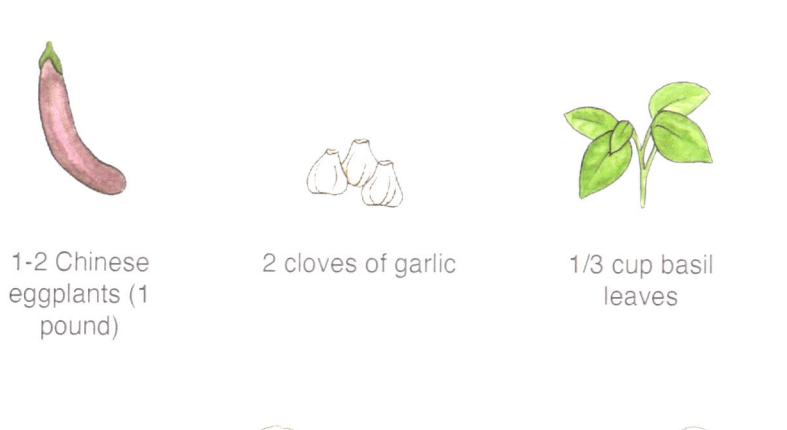

1-2 Chinese eggplants (1 pound)

2 cloves of garlic

1/3 cup basil leaves

Cilantro or green onion for garnish

1 tbsp chili bean sauce

1 tsp sugar

2 tbsp cooking oil

3 tbsp + 1/4 cup water, separated

1 tbsp soy sauce

1 Cut the eggplant into 1.5-inch sections, then halve or quarter each section depending on the thickness of the eggplant. For each section, cut slits on the white side to help it cook through.

2 Add 3 tbsp water and 1 tbsp oil in a large, flat pan and lay the eggplant skin side up across the pan in a single layer. Cover the pan, turn on high heat and cook for 5 minutes without opening the lid.

3 Remove the pan from the stove, take out the eggplant and plate them. Return pan to stove.

4 Heat 1 tbsp oil, then add garlic, chili sauce, soy sauce, sugar, and 1/4 cup water. Cook until sauce is bubbling. Toss in basil. Turn off heat and pour sauce on top of eggplant. Garnish with green onion and/or cilantro.

THE JENG GUIDE TO GREENS

Taiwanese cooking is very veggie forward and leafy greens are a staple of any meal. There are tons of options you'll find at any Asian grocery store (and even more when you visit the home country), but these four are the favorites of the Jeng family. Most of the time we cook these simply with a hot wok, minced garlic and cooking oil and it turns out delicious. Below are some tasting notes and cooking variations to build these into your dinner rotation.

Yu Choy
油菜 | Yóucài

There are many types of 'choys' you'll find at the Asian grocery store, but I like Yu Choy as it has the classic flavor and crunch but is less stringy and more bite-sized compared to bok choy.
Tastes like: Sweet and slightly bitter (in the mustard family), like a cross between broccoli and spinach.
Cook with: garlic & oil; oyster sauce

Pea Shoots
豆苗 | Dòu miáo

These are truly one of our all-time favorite side greens - the rich flavor is unlike any other, but it also costs 4-5x other vegetables (and is often more expensive than meat).
Tastes like: Buttery and rich, crunchy and tender with a slightly sweet flavor profile.
Cook with: lots of garlic and oil on high heat

Water Spinach
空心菜 | Kōngxīncài

Water spinach is known for its distinctive hollow stem (which helps make it tender) and was one of Nai Nai's favorite vegetables to cook. They are easy to find and one of the more cost efficient veggies.
Tastes like: Slightly savory, nutty flavor with tender shoots.
Cook with: garlic and oil; fermented tofu

Mustard Greens
芥菜 | Jiè cài

Mustard greens can be very polarizing due to their bitterness. These veggies can be prepared 'fresh' as a side dish or pickled and added as an accoutrement to other dishes (see recipe).
Tastes like: Bitter, mustard-y (shocking), crunchy stalks with tender leaves.
Cook with: garlic and oil

MAIN DISHES

CHIVE BOX

韭菜盒子 | Jiǔcài hézi

Serving Size: 6

The literal translation of this dish is 'chive box', but it's really more of an Asian hot pocket. We make lots of these when chives are in season, then freeze them for a lil snack whenever we're craving that fragrant chive flavor.

 1/2 pound of chives

 1 bundle bean thread vermicelli (about 38 mg)

 8 oz bean curd

 1 tbsp small dried shrimp

 1 egg, beaten

 1/8 tsp + 1 tsp salt, separated

 1 tsp pepper

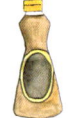 1/2 tsp sesame oil

 1-1/4 cup flour

 1/3 cup + 2 tbsp water

 1/4 tsp active dry yeast

1 Mix flour, water, yeast, 1/8 tsp salt and knead. Form a ball, cover with a damp cloth, and prove for 1.5 hours.

2 Soak vermicelli in a bowl of water for 30 minutes. Soak dried shrimp in warm water for 10 minutes.

3 Scramble the egg in a frying pan. Break the egg up into small bits with a wooden spoon.

4 Chop bean curd, dried shrimp and chives into small 1/2-cm cubes. Cut vermicelli into 2 cm long pieces.

5 Mix chives, vermicelli, bean curd, dried shrimp, scrambled egg, 1 tsp salt, pepper, and sesame oil together in a large bowl.

6 Divide dough into six parts and roll each out into a large 8" circle. With each dough circle, spoon over half of it with the chive filling, then fold the dough and press down on the edges to seal it.

7 Cook right away or freeze for later. To cook, heat up some oil in a wide, shallow pan. Cook the chive box for several minutes on each side until golden brown. Slice and serve hot.

LION'S HEAD MEATBALL SOUP

獅子頭 | Shīzitóu

Serving Size: 6

This dish is a longstanding family favorite that is so comforting and easy enough to make. During COVID, we had an impromptu family cooking contest where we all created this dish on our own and sent each other photos and commentary on (perceived) taste, ingredients, and presentation. It ended up being a four-way tie for first place, but as the unofficial tie-breaker, I can tell you this recipe here is the true winner.

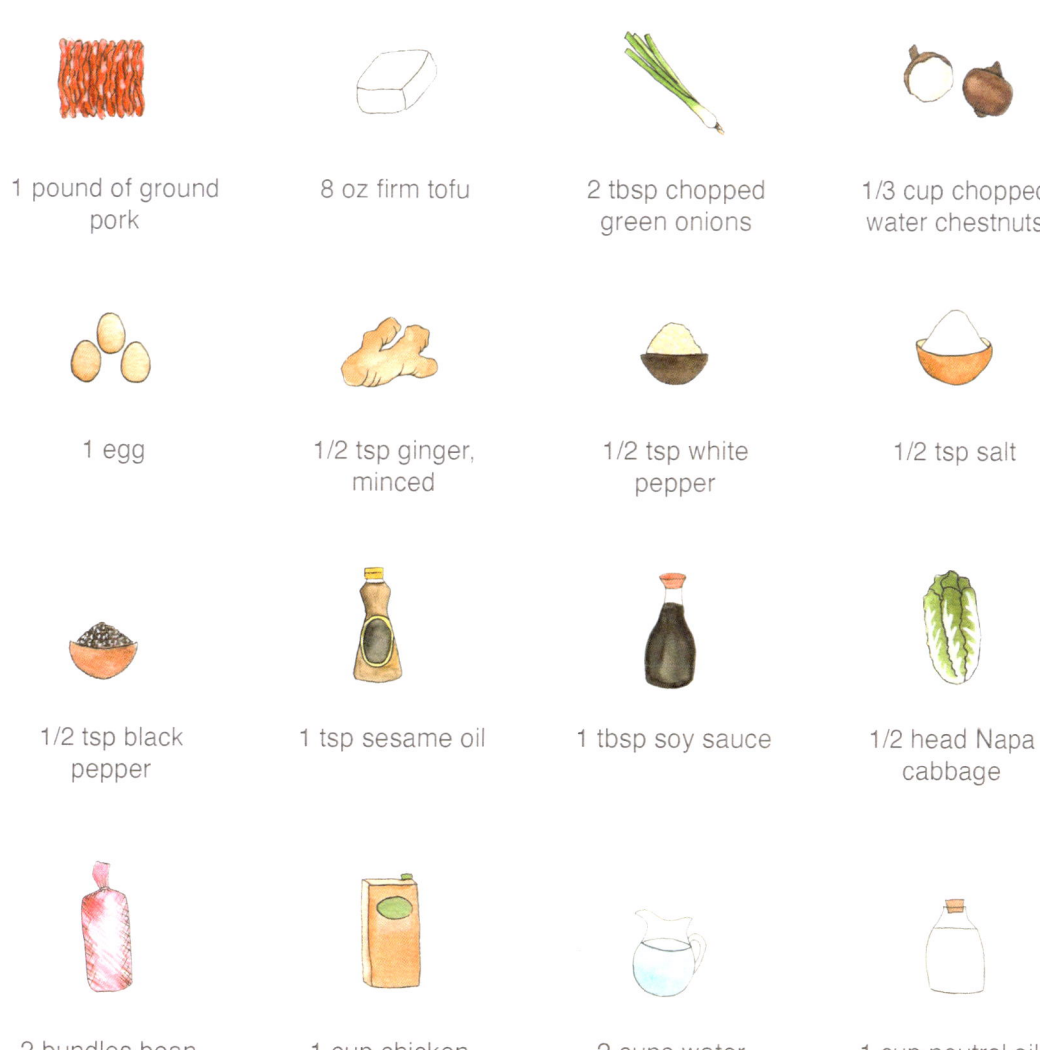

- 1 pound of ground pork
- 8 oz firm tofu
- 2 tbsp chopped green onions
- 1/3 cup chopped water chestnuts
- 1 egg
- 1/2 tsp ginger, minced
- 1/2 tsp white pepper
- 1/2 tsp salt
- 1/2 tsp black pepper
- 1 tsp sesame oil
- 1 tbsp soy sauce
- 1/2 head Napa cabbage
- 2 bundles bean thread vermicelli (~76 mg)
- 1 cup chicken broth
- 2 cups water
- 1 cup neutral oil for frying

1 In a large bowl, marinate pork in sesame oil, soy sauce, salt, white pepper, black pepper, and ginger for 10 minutes.

2 Combine marinated pork with tofu, green onion, water chestnuts, and egg. Make sure to mush up the tofu so it's dispersed throughout the meatball (no large chunks of tofu). The easiest way to do this is with your hands - so get messy!

3 Shape into large 2-inch meatballs and lay them on a plate as you go.

4 Heat up frying oil in a large pot and fry the meatballs in oil, turning as it browns on each side. This should take a few minutes per meatball.

5 Soak vermicelli in water for 20 minutes.

6 Wash and chop the cabbage into large flat chunks.

7 In a large cast iron or clay pot, pan-fry the cabbage in a couple of tablespoons of the frying oil for a few minutes to help sear in the flavor.

8 Add chicken broth and 2 cups of water. Place the meatballs on top of the cabbage and bring to a boil. Reduce heat, add vermicelli threads, and cook for 20 minutes.

9 Serve on its own as a stew or over rice for a heartier meal.

MAPO TOFU

麻婆豆腐 | Má pó dòufu

Serving Size: 4

Mapo tofu is one of those dishes that is pretty universally loved. It's flavorful but simple, it's got some meat but isn't a meat-heavy dish and it's spicy but not uncontrollably so. This is mom's go-to, quick-fire recipe she uses when she has a package of tofu in the fridge and some extra ground pork.

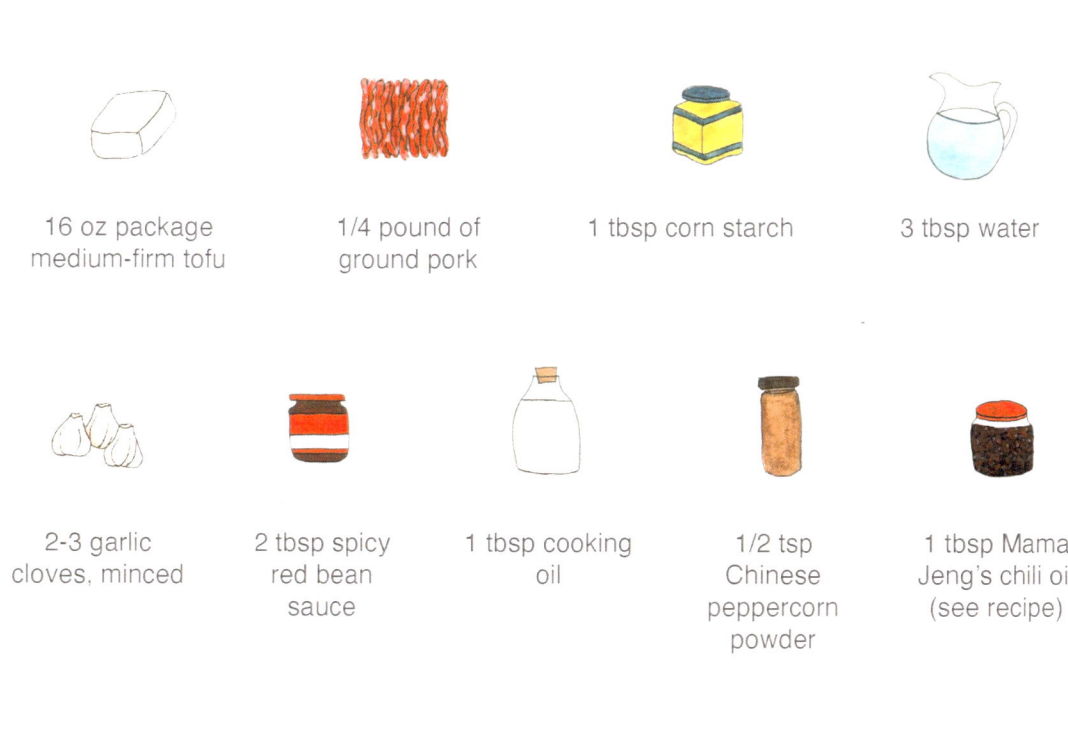

16 oz package medium-firm tofu

1/4 pound of ground pork

1 tbsp corn starch

3 tbsp water

2-3 garlic cloves, minced

2 tbsp spicy red bean sauce

1 tbsp cooking oil

1/2 tsp Chinese peppercorn powder

1 tbsp Mama Jeng's chili oil (see recipe)

1. Cut tofu into dice-sized cubes. Place them on a paper towel for 15 minutes to soak up excess water.

2. Saute minced garlic with oil in a hot pan. Add ground pork and fry until it's dry, crumbly and a little brown.

3. Add spicy red bean sauce, chili oil and tofu. Stir well.

4. Mix corn starch with water in a small bowl. Pour into tofu mixture to thicken.

5. Serve over rice with a sprinkle of Chinese peppercorn powder.

PORK & SHRIMP WONTONS

馄饨 | Húntún

Serving Size: 6

Wontons were my favorite dish growing up. The recipe below is a classic version we'd often create, but there were variations from time to time - subbing in vegetables like cabbage. This (like many other dishes in this cookbook) can easily be frozen for later or eaten fresh. They can also be made as a soup or with a spicy sesame sauce.

| 1/2 pound of ground pork | 1/2 pound of shrimp | 1/2 tsp ginger, minced | 1/4 cup water chestnuts, minced | 2 tbsp green onions, chopped |

  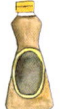 

| 1/4 tsp black pepper | 1/2 tsp salt | 1 tsp sesame oil | 14 oz package wonton skins |

MAKING THE FILLING

1. Marinate ground pork in sesame oil, salt, pepper and ginger for 10 minutes.

2. Wash, peel and de-vein shrimp. Chop into pea-sized pieces.

3. In a large bowl, mix pork, shrimp, water chestnuts, and green onions together.

WRAPPING INSTRUCTIONS

1. Place a teaspoon of filling into the center of the wonton skin and wet the edges with water.

2. Fold the wonton skin in half in a triangle and press the edges tightly to seal shut.

3. Twist one flap in front of the other to create the wonton shape.

4. Pinch the flaps together with water to cinch them in place. Make sure the wontons are sealed well or the filling will fall out when you're cooking.

WONTON SOUP

Enjoy your wontons in a comforting soup with your favorite veggies. Heat up a pot with a 1:2 ratio of chicken broth to water. Add wontons, Napa cabbage, a few slices of ginger, green onions and anything else you want!

WONTONS WITH SPICY SESAME SAUCE

For a richer, more savory meal, try wontons with a creamy sesame sauce. Assemble sauce in a bowl - for a single serving, use 1 tbsp sweet sesame paste, 1/4 tsp sesame oil, 1/2 tsp soy sauce, 1/4 tsp Mama Jeng's chili oil (see recipe) and 2 tbsp hot water. Boil about 10 wontons in water, then strain and mix the hot wontons directly in the serving bowl with the sauce.

SAVORY STEAMED BUNS
包子 | Bāozi

Serving Size: 24 buns

The base for this recipe can be used with just about any sort of bao filling, including the dim sum favorite - char siu bao. Growing up, we'd make these in large batches, eat some while it was fresh out of the steamer and freeze the rest. These keep well and are a super convenient snack or a lazy weeknight meal. After steaming, you could also pan-fry these to get a nice crisp texture, and enjoy with Mama Jeng's famous chili crisp (see recipe).

3-1/4 cup flour

1-1/4 cup milk

2 tsp active dry yeast

1 tbsp cooking oil

1/8 cup sugar

DOUGH PREPARATION

1. Heat a half cup of the milk and mix in the sugar to dissolve it. Add in the remaining milk so that it becomes lukewarm.

2. Add yeast and let it sit for 3-5 minutes. It should be frothing a little at this point.

3. Add milk and yeast mixture to flour along with oil and knead in a stand mixer for 8 minutes.

4. Roll dough into a large ball and cover with a damp towel. Prove in a warm place for one hour until it's doubled in size.

5. Using a kitchen scale, separate dough into 24 equally sized balls.

6. With a rolling pin, roll out each ball into a ~5-inch pancake. Pro move: make the edges of the pancake thinner and keep the middle thicker. This will come in handy when assembling the bao.

MAKING THE FILLING

There is an unlimited combination of savory or sweet fillings you could concoct to put inside these buns. Below are four of my favorite savory bun fillings. Mix these up in a large bowl along with the staples (sesame oil, ginger, soy sauce, salt and pepper) and assemble your buns!

CLASSIC PORK & CABBAGE	GREEN BEAN & PORK	CHAR SIU PORK	CHIVES & TOFU
 1 pound of ground pork	 1-1/2 pound of green beans, boiled and diced	 1-1/2 pound of char siu pork, diced	 1/2 pound of chives, chopped into small pieces
 1 pound Napa cabbage, sweated and chopped	 1 pound of ground pork  1/2 cup green onions, chopped	 1 tbsp corn starch mixed with a bit of water	 8 oz bean curd tofu, diced finely  1 bundle bean thread vermicelli, chopped (~38mg)

 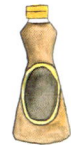  

+ 1 tsp sesame oil | 1 tsp grated ginger | 2 tsp soy sauce | Salt & pepper to taste

WRAPPING INSTRUCTIONS

1   Add a large spoonful of filling into the middle of the dough.

2   Pull the sides up and pinch and gather as you go, using your thumb to push the filling inwards. Seal the bao at the top tightly. Once sealed, give it a final twist for dramatic effect.

3   Dab the bottom of the bao with a bit of cooking oil and set it on a small piece of wax paper. This will help prevent it from sticking to the steamer after cooking.

COOKING

4 Arrange the bao in a steamer with 1.5 inches to spare around each bao. Let the bao prove for another 20 minutes.

5 Start boiling your steamer water, then steam bao for 13 minutes. Remove from heat and serve fresh, with Mama Jeng's chili oil. Alt: pan-fry the bao in a skillet with oil for a crispy texture.

PAN-FRIED COD WITH CHILI OIL

香煎鱈魚 | Xiāngjiān xuěyú

Serving Size: 2

Black cod or sea bass makes for a great main dish as it's hearty and also tender. It's also hard to overcook, so it's fairly idiot-proof as far as fish dishes go. This recipe is super simple but packed with a lot of flavor and always a great addition to a nice family-style meal.

1 pound of black cod or sea bass

1 tbsp ginger, peeled and sliced

1 chili pepper, sliced

1 clove garlic, sliced

1 tsp sugar

2 tbsp soy sauce

3 tbsp cooking oil

1. De-scale sea bass, leaving the skin on. Pro tip: do this in water if you can, otherwise the scales go everywhere. I once found a scale in my hair the next day in the shower. Don't be me.

2. Heat oil in a wok or pan. Sauté some ginger slices until fragrant, then remove from pan.

3. Pan fry the fish in oil and cook through until it starts to flake. When fish is done, plate it and set it aside.

4. In the remaining oil, cook the pepper and garlic for 2 minutes.

5. Add sugar and soy sauce to the pan and mix it up. Then pour over the fish on the plate.

STICKY RICE DUMPLINGS
粽子 | Zòngzi

Serving Size: 20 dumplings

Also known as "Chinese Tamales", these sticky rice dumplings are traditionally made during the dragon boat festival. We don't make this very often but whenever we do, it's a day of prep and a whole family affair. Most of the time spent on this recipe involves advance prep for the filling ingredients. The assembly and cooking itself is relatively quick and always fun to do, with family members gathered around and wrapping dumplings together.

40 bamboo leaves

1 pound of pork shoulder

10 rice cups of sticky rice (7.5 regular cups)

10 dried shiitake mushrooms

1 cup of peanuts, de-shelled

2 cups taro, chopped into 1-inch chunks

1/4 cup dried shrimp

1 tbsp dry fried shallots

1/3 cup soy sauce

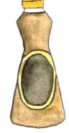

1/4 cup sesame oil

1/4 cup grapeseed oil

1 tsp pepper

8 oz chicken broth

76

ADVANCE PREP

1. The night before: soak bamboo leaves in water with a heavy bowl to submerge and weigh it down. 40 leaves will make 20 rice dumplings.

2. Soak 10 rice cups (7.5 regular cups) of sticky rice in water for at least 4 hours.

INGREDIENT PREP

3. After soaking the bamboo leaves, give each leaf a light scrub with a soft sponge, then dry with a clean towel.

4. Cook rice on the stove top for 5-10 minutes with chicken broth, soy sauce, sesame oil, grapeseed oil and fried shallots. The rice will be partially cooked but not fully.

5. Cut the pork into 1-inch chunks and cook in a wok or fry pan until cooked through.

6. Boil the peanuts for 5 minutes and drain. Set aside.

7. Soak shiitake mushrooms for 15 minutes, then slice into strips.

8. Soak the dried shrimp in hot water for 15 minutes, then drain. Set aside.

9. Cut taro into 1-inch chunks and cook in a wok or fry pan for 5-10 minutes. It will be partially, but not completely, cooked through.

10. Prepare all the ingredients in separate bowls for easy assembly. Plan on the following amount for each dumpling: 1/3 cup sticky rice, 1 piece pork, 1 piece taro chunk, 1/2 shiitake mushroom, 2-3 shrimp, 4-5 peanuts.

11. Cut 10 4-foot strands of bakers twine. Take five strands and fold in half making a loop knot at the top to make bundles of ten.

WRAPPING INSTRUCTIONS

1 Take two bamboo leaves and fold one end up at an angle.

2 Bend back the folded part to make a pocket (the bottom corner should overlap slightly).

3 Hold it upright in the palm of your hand for ease of stuffing.

4 Add a spoonful of rice and stuff it down. Add the ingredients (see previous page), pressing down each time. Then top with another 2 spoonfuls of rice.

5 Fold down on the sides to start to cover the stuffing, making the rice compact.

6 Press as you bring the sides closer together, keeping the sides taut.

7 Fold over the top flap to fully cover the stuffing.

8 Once the dumpling is compact and completely covered with the bamboo leaves, wrap a piece of twine around the dumpling tightly and tie a knot.

9 At the end, you should have two bundles of ten dumplings each.

COOKING INSTRUCTIONS

10 Bring a large steamer of water to a boil.

11 Add dumplings and steam for 45 minutes to an hour. Check halfway through to make sure there's enough water.

12 Unwrap and enjoy while hot and fresh! Serve with sweet chili sauce for a little kick.

STIR-FRIED RICE CAKES WITH MUSTARD GREENS

雪菜炒年糕 | Xuě cài chǎo niángāo

Serving Size: 4

The first time I made this dish, I was told it didn't really count because I didn't pickle my own mustard greens. Now, thanks to the handy pickled mustard greens recipe (also included in this book), this dish can come together easily and with all homemade ingredients.

1 cup pickled mustard greens (see recipe)

1 package of rice cakes (16 oz)

1/4 pound of pork loin

1 chili pepper

1 tsp soy sauce

1 tsp corn starch

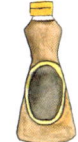
1 tsp sesame oil

1 tbsp cooking oil

1 tsp salt

1/4 tsp pepper

1. Cut pork into small strips, then marinate in soy sauce, pepper and sesame oil for 15 minutes. Sprinkle with corn starch and mix.

2. Boil a pot of water, drop rice cakes in and cook for 2 minutes. Strain and toss with a bit of oil to prevent sticking.

3. In a hot wok, heat up some cooking oil and stir-fry the pork. Then add mustard greens and chili pepper and cook for 3 minutes.

4. Add rice cakes and toss. Salt to taste. Serve hot.

SALTED CRISPY FISH
鹽酥魚 | Yán sū yú

Serving Size: 4

This dish has similar flavors and vibes to the popular Taiwanese salted crispy chicken (or popcorn chicken, depending on who you ask). Most of the process in this recipe is the marinade and sauce preparation. The actual fish fry is relatively simply (no egg wash needed!) and the flavors from the marinade really make it stand out.

 1 pound of tilapia fillets

 2 tbsp soy sauce

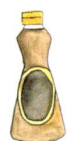 1 tsp sesame oil

 1/2 tsp each salt and pepper

 2 cloves garlic, sliced

 1/2 tsp sugar

 2 tsp Taiwanese black vinegar

 1 tsp Shaoxing wine

 1/2 tsp five-spice powder

 1/2 cup sweet potato flour

1 Create the marinade in a bowl by whisking together soy sauce, sesame oil, salt, pepper, black vinegar, sugar, wine, five-spice powder and garlic.

2 Cut tilapia fillets into 1x2-inch pieces. Soak the tilapia in the marinade for at least 20 minutes.

3 Pour sweet potato flour in a shallow bowl. Dredge tilapia pieces in the flour and arrange on a plate. Let it sit for 15 minutes to absorb the coating.

4 Fry fish in 1/2 cup cooking oil, turning after 1-2 minutes on each side.

5 Optional Sauce: Mix 2 tbsp soy sauce, 2 tbsp lemon juice, 1 tbsp sugar, 1 tbsp fish sauce, 2 tbsp water, 1 tbsp sesame oil, a pinch of Chinese peppercorn powder, minced cilantro, jalapeño pepper and garlic. Mix all the ingredients and pour over fish after frying.

FIVE SPICE PORK WITH RICE

滷肉飯 | Lǔ ròu fàn

Serving Size: 8

Five-spice pork over rice (or Lu Rou Fan) is a classic and popular Taiwanese dish. But as I've grown up, I've learned the Lu Rou Fan I've always known is actually pretty unique to our family. I like to say that it's 'fully-loaded'. When you order this dish in Taiwan, it often comes as a small bowl on the side with just the pork over rice. When we make it at home, we load it up with eggs, tofu, mushrooms and make a large batch, enough for several family meals.

1-1/2 pound of pork belly with skin on (alt: ground pork) | 8 eggs | 12 oz fried tofu, (1-inch cubes) | 3-4 dried shiitake mushrooms

2 tbsp shallot, minced | 1 tsp ginger, minced | 1 tbsp garlic, minced | 1 tsp sugar or 3 pieces rock sugar

1/3 cup dark soy sauce | 1/4 cup regular soy sauce | 2 tbsp white wine | 1-1/2 cup chicken broth

 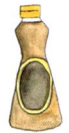  

1/2 cup water | 1 tbsp sesame oil | Salt and pepper to taste | 1 tsp five-spice powder

1   Chop pork belly into small dice-sized pieces.

2   Place dried shiitake mushrooms in warm water and let it soak for 15-20 minutes, then dice into small pieces.

3   Bring a pot of water to a boil. Place eggs in and boil for 10 minutes. When eggs are done, remove them from hot water, let cool, then peel.

4   Using the same hot water in the pan, boil the tofu in water for 2-3 minutes.

5   In a large frying pan, sauté the shallots in sesame oil until caramelized. Add garlic and ginger and cook for 1-2 minutes. Add pork to the frying pan and cook until browned.

6   Combine all prepared ingredients in a large pot. Make sure there is enough liquid to just cover the ingredients. If not, add a bit more water and/or soy sauce.

7   Bring to a boil, then reduce to simmer and cook for 2 hours. In the meantime, prepare rice in your rice cooker.

8   Salt and pepper to taste and enjoy over rice!

PICKLED LONG BEAN HASH VERMICELLI

肉末豇豆 | Ròu mò jiāngdòu

Serving Size: 4

Technically this long bean hash can go with anything, like on rice or in a lettuce cup. But this pairing with vermicelli and the poached egg on top makes it a nice hearty one bowl meal. This is a dish that has been re-imagined by my mom and is packed full of flavors.

1 cup pickled long beans, diced (see recipe) | 2 cups cabbage, diced | 1/2 cup carrots, diced | 2 chili peppers, diced

1/2 pound of ground pork | 4 eggs | 6 oz vermicelli rice noodles | 1/2 tsp + 1/2 tsp salt, separated | 1/4 tsp + 1/4 tsp pepper, separated

 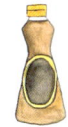  

1 tbsp cooking oil | 1 tsp sesame oil | 2 tsp soy sauce | Mama Jeng's chili oil (see recipe) | 1/2 tsp + 1/2 tsp sugar, separated

1. Cook the ground pork with 1/2 tsp sugar, 1/2 tsp salt, 1/4 tsp pepper in the pan until browned. Set aside.

2. Stir-fry the pickled long beans in 1 tbsp oil in a wok for 2 minutes, Then add 2 cups of water and cook for 10 minutes or until cooked through.

3. Add carrots and cook for 3 minutes. Then add chili peppers, cabbage and cook for an additional 5 minutes. Add ground pork back in and season with 1/2 tsp salt, 1/2 tsp sugar, 1 tsp sesame oil, 1/4 tsp pepper.

4. Bring a pot of water to a boil, then cook vermicelli for 1-3 minutes, as instructed on the packaging. Remove vermicelli with tongs, leaving the boiling water.

5. Crack eggs into a sieve in the boiling water for 4 minutes to poach them.

6. Assemble bowls with vermicelli layer on the bottom. Spoon the pickled long bean hash over the vermicelli, and top with the poached egg. Then spoon 1-2 ladles of hot water (can use the boiling water from the vermicelli) into each bowl.

7. Add seasoning to the soup to taste - soy sauce, sesame oil, chili oil, salt. Mix and enjoy!

POT STICKER DUMPLINGS
鍋貼 | Guōtiē

Serving Size: 60 dumplings

These dumplings can take a bit of time to make, but they keep well (in the freezer, of course) and are a great easy dinner on a rainy or lazy day. This recipe makes a ton at once, so it easily covers multiple meals for multiple people. Pro tip: make it a party and get other people to help fold the dumplings. You can get creative so long as it gets sealed in the end. It's also worth noting that these dumplings can be boiled or pan-fried, but in this recipe, we're making the crispy pot sticker version.

1/2 pound of shrimp, peeled and diced

1 pound of Napa cabbage, diced

3/4 pound of ground pork

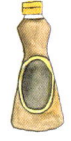
1 tsp sesame oil

1 tsp soy sauce

1/4 tsp pepper

1 tsp salt

1 tsp ginger, minced

16 oz pack of dumpling wrappers

2 tbsp neutral cooking oil

WRAPPING INSTRUCTIONS

1. Marinate pork in sesame oil, soy sauce, salt, and pepper for 5 minutes. Mix meat, shrimp, cabbage, and ginger together in a large bowl using your hands to thoroughly mix as needed.

2. Place a tablespoon of filling in the middle of a dumpling wrapper and wet the edges of the wrapper with water.

3. Fold the wrapper in half and pinch to close at the top.

4. Starting on one side, fold over part of the wrapper towards the middle and pinch to seal. Do this 2-3 more times on that side, depending on how many folds you want in your dumpling.

5. Repeat the process in reverse on the other side, folding towards the middle each time.

COOKING INSTRUCTIONS

6. Add 2 tbsp oil to a large flat non-stick plan. Place dumplings in the pot, then pour enough water to almost cover them.

7. Place lid on the pan and cook on medium heat until the water has cooked through and there is a crispy blackened layer at the bottom of the pan.

8. Using a spatula, gently lift the pot stickers (they may be stuck together - embrace it!). Serve with chili oil and soy sauce and enjoy while warm!

MOUTHWATERING CHICKEN
口水鷄 | Kǒushuǐ jī

Serving Size: 4

The literal translation of this dish is 'saliva chicken' which is super gross, but fairly accurate as this dish is full of flavor and umami. My mom's version is extra yummy as she uses chicken drumsticks (moist, flavorful and rich), cucumbers (for a bit of crisp freshness) and her homemade chili oil.

1 pound of chicken drumsticks

2 Persian cucumbers, cut into spears

2 tbsp ginger, sliced

2 stalks of green onions, chopped

2 tbsp Szechuan peppercorn

1 tbsp salt

1 tsp sugar

1 tbsp Mama Jeng's chili oil (see recipe)

2 tbsp soy sauce

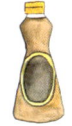

1 tsp sesame oil

1/4 cup white cooking wine

2 tbsp cooking oil

1 Heat a large pot of water with 1 tbsp of ginger, 1 stalk of green onion and wine. Boil the drumsticks for 15 minutes until cooked through. Remove chicken and place in a bowl of ice water to cool.

2 Sprinkle cut cucumbers with salt and let it sweat for 15 minutes. Rinse off the salt and squeeze the water out of the cucumbers.

3 Start making the sauce in a small bowl by mixing soy sauce, sesame oil, sugar and chili oil. Set aside.

4 Heat oil in a wok or pan and cook the Szechuan peppercorn until it just starts to smoke. Remove the peppercorns. Add ginger and onion and cook for an additional minute.

5 Pour hot oil into the bowl with the rest of the ingredients and whisk together.

6 Pull the chicken meat off the bones. Plate cucumbers, layer chicken on top. Pour sauce over the dish and serve at room temperature.

MUSHU GREEN ONION PANCAKE STIR-FRY

木須炒餅 | Mùxū chǎo bǐng

Serving Size: 2

This dish is a crowd pleaser and in my case, a husband pleaser. It's got all the best parts of Chinese cooking - veggie forward, just a bit of meat for protein and flavor, stir-fried goodness and of course, green onion pancakes. This can be a side dish but we'll usually make this and devour it between the two of us as a one pot meal. Enjoy!

1/2 cup woodear mushrooms

1 large carrot

2 cups cabbage, shredded

1/2 large yellow onion, sliced

6 oz pork loin, cut into thin strips

1/2 tsp salt

2 green onion pancakes (see recipe)

1. Pan fry 2 green onion pancakes until golden brown. Let cool, then cut or chop into narrow strips. Set aside.

2. Cut onion into slices. Saute in pan with oil until translucent and browned. Add in carrots and cook for 3 minutes.

3. Add pork loins and cook through, about 4 minutes.

4. Add shredded cabbage and woodear mushrooms and cook for 4 minutes. Season with salt.

5. Lastly, add the green onion pancake strips and toss to mix. Serve warm.

BOILED CHIVE, PORK & SQUASH DUMPLINGS

水餃 | Shuǐjiǎo

Serving Size: 4

This dumpling recipe can work for any type of savory filling. The main difference between this and the pot sticker dumpling recipe is the wrapper (boiled dumplings should use thinner wrappers) and preparation style (boiled vs. pan-fried). It's also more critical for the dumplings to be fully sealed when boiling lest the fillings fall out of their lil' pockets.

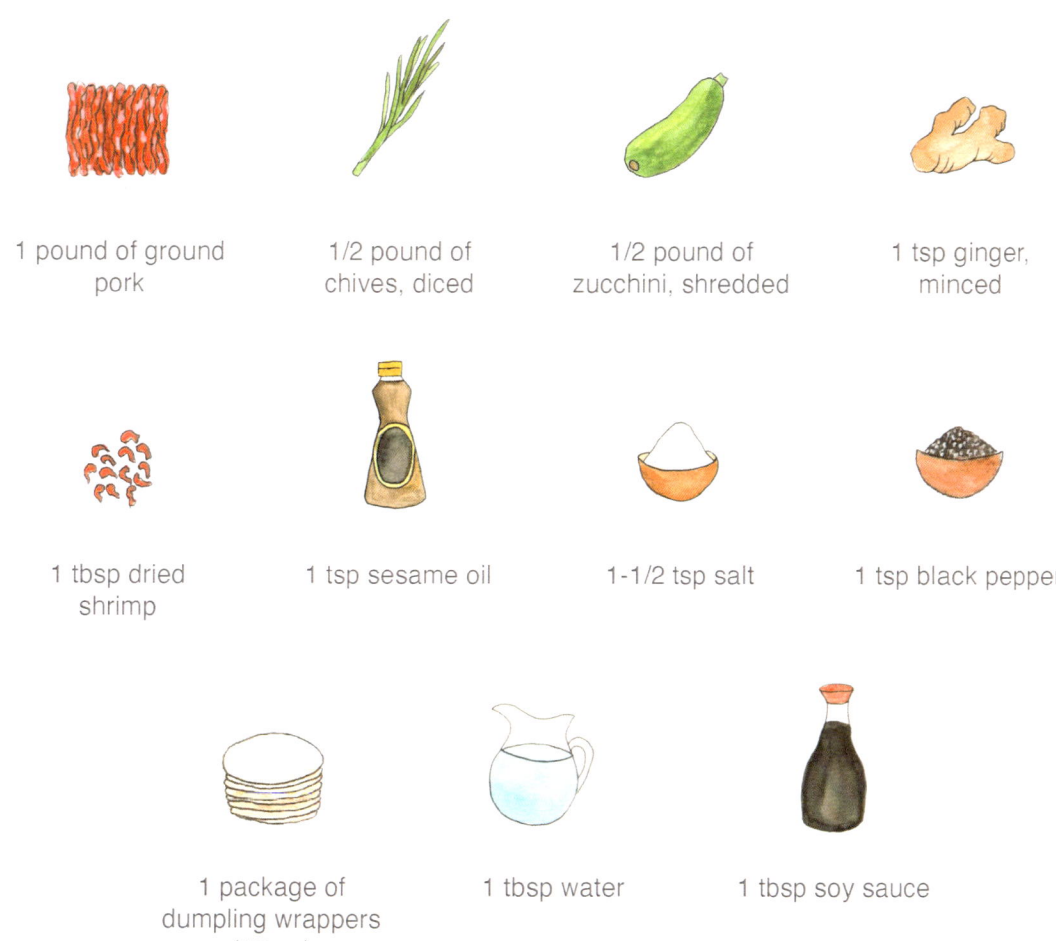

1 pound of ground pork

1/2 pound of chives, diced

1/2 pound of zucchini, shredded

1 tsp ginger, minced

1 tbsp dried shrimp

1 tsp sesame oil

1-1/2 tsp salt

1 tsp black pepper

1 package of dumpling wrappers (16 oz)

1 tbsp water

1 tbsp soy sauce

FILLING & WRAPPING INSTRUCTIONS

1 Soak dried shrimp in warm water for 10 minutes. Once soaked through, remove from water and mince shrimp.

2 Mince ginger and add 1 tbsp water. Let it soak for a few minutes.

3 Shred the zucchini with a medium-sized grater and wring out the water. Dice chives into small pieces.

4 Season the ground pork with soy sauce, pepper, sesame oil and salt.

5 Add ginger water and minced shrimp to the meat and mix thoroughly. Then add the shredded zucchini and chopped chives.

6 Assemble the dumplings according to the same wrapping instructions as the pot sticker dumplings (see page 90).

COOKING INSTRUCTIONS

7 Bring a large pot of water to a boil. Place the dumplings in and boil for 6-7 minutes. Remove with a sieve or strainer.

8 Serve hot with a dipping sauce of soy sauce, vinegar, and chili oil.

COLD SESAME NOODLES

涼麵 | Liáng miàn

Serving Size: 3-4

Cold sesame noodles are popular street food in Taiwan and always at the top of my list when I visit. This dish is one of my summertime favorites. It's flavorful, refreshing and full of yummy textures thanks to the soft noodles and crunch of the carrots and cucumbers.

8 oz thin noodles

1/3 cup cucumber, julienned

1/3 cup carrots, julienned

2 eggs, beaten

3 tbsp sweet sesame paste

1 tbsp Mama Jeng's chili oil (see recipe)

1/4 cup water

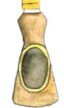
1 tsp sesame oil, separated

1 tsp rice wine vinegar

1 tbsp soy sauce

1-1/2 tsp salt

1/2 tsp pepper

1 clove garlic, grated

1. Boil the noodles according to package instructions. When done, run immediately under cold water until noodles are cooled, then toss with 1 tsp sesame oil to prevent stickiness.

2. Fry the egg, pancake-style – letting it cook completely on one side before flipping it over. Cool, then fold into thirds and slice into thin strips.

3. To prepare the sauce, mix sesame paste, water, chili oil, sesame oil, salt, pepper, garlic, and rice wine vinegar.

4. Pour sauce over noodles and mix well – it should be extra saucy to cover the vegetables once added.

5. Top noodles with sliced egg, carrots and cucumber – then serve cold!

DAD'S FAMOUS BEEF NOODLE SOUP

牛肉麵 | Niúròu miàn

Serving Size: 8

My mom has long been known as the chef of the household but when it comes to the Taiwanese classic dish, beef noodle soup, my dad reigns supreme. This recipe has taken him years to perfect. It's not a quick dish (nor should it be), but as an expert beef noodle soup consumer, I can tell you it is worth the wait.

3 pounds of beef bones

1 Chinese spice packet (see recipe for substitutions)

3 tbsp ginger slices, separated

2 stalks of green onions, chopped and separated

2 star anise pods

1-1/2 pound of beef shank

3 large tomatoes

1 clove garlic, minced

1/4 cup + 2 tbsp red wine

1/4 cup regular soy sauce

1/4 cup dark soy sauce

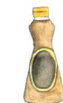

1/4 tsp sesame oil

1/4 tsp black pepper

1/4 tsp white pepper

2 tbsp spicy red bean sauce

1/2 tsp sugar

1 tbsp cooking oil

2 dried hot chili peppers

2 16-oz packages of dried noodles

1 cup pickled mustard greens (see recipe)

1. Use some bakers twine to wrap the beef shank tightly. This helps ensure that the beef remains tender while cooking.

2. Put beef bones, beef shank, 1 stalk green onion, 2-3 slices of ginger, dried chili peppers, spice packet and star anise into a large stockpot and cover with water. Bring to a boil, then reduce to medium and cook for one hour. Note: If you want to make your own spice packet, use 1-1/2 tsp fennel, 1 cinnamon stick, pinch of ground cumin, an additional 2 slices of ginger, 1-1/2 tsp cloves and place in a spice sack.

3. In the meantime, bring a small pot of water to a boil and cook the tomatoes until the skin wrinkles. Peel the skin off and chop into rough quarters.

4. In a small bowl, mix together soy sauce, dark soy sauce, black pepper, white pepper, sesame oil, sugar and 2 tbsp red wine to make a sauce. Set aside.

5. When the beef has been cooking for an hour, remove the beef shank and cut off the twine. Slice the beef into 1/4-inch slices.

6. Heat up a skillet with a bit of cooking oil. Sauté garlic, 1 stalk green onion, 2 tbsp sliced ginger until oil is fragrant. Then add sliced beef and saute for 2 minutes. Add tomatoes and the sauce mixture and cook for 3 more minutes.

7. Pour the contents of the skillet into the stockpot and cook on low for another 2-3 hours. At that point, the soup portion is done! You can enjoy immediately (see next steps) or save it for when you're ready to eat, at which point you'll cook the noodles and veggies.

8. Boil noodles according to package. Strain noodles and separate into 8 bowls. Ladle soup on top of noodles, then top with a heaping spoonful of pickled mustard greens. Serve hot and don't forget to slurp while you eat!

"CHINESE SPAGHETTI"
炸醬麵 | Zhá jiàng miàn

Serving Size: 4

There are many names for this classic Chinese dish – Zha Jiang Mian, Chinese Fried Sauce noodles, Spicy Pork noodles, etc. Growing up in the Jeng family, however, this dish was most commonly known as Chinese Spaghetti. The Jeng recipe is a bit more savory and thicker than other variations, with a lot of delicately diced tofu and crunchy cucumber.

1/2 pound of ground pork

1 stalk green onion, minced

8 oz dried bean curd, diced finely

4 tbsp sweet black bean sauce

1 tbsp soy sauce

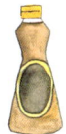
1 tsp sesame oil

12 oz dried noodles

1 tsp corn starch

1 cup water

Salt and pepper, to taste

2 Persian cucumbers, Jullenned

1. Heat up sesame oil in a pan or wok, add the green onions and cook for one minute.

2. Add ground pork and cook until browned, breaking up the meat into small pieces as you cook. Add diced soy bean curd and cook for an additional 2 minutes. Add black bean sauce, soy sauce, salt and pepper. Cook on high heat for 3-4 minutes.

3. In a small bowl, mix water with corn starch. Pour into meat and tofu sauce on the stove and stir well. Remove from heat.

4. Boil noodles and strain. Spoon sauce over the hot noodles. Garnish with sliced cucumber. Add Mama Jeng's chili oil for a little extra kick. Enjoy!

DRINKS & DESSERTS

BLACK SESAME PANNA COTTA
黑芝麻奶酪 | Hēi zhīma nǎilào

Serving Size: 4

This delicious dessert is a classic example of mom's fusion recipes, using black sesame flavors common in Asian desserts with the rich creamy decadence of a classic panna cotta. I'll admit, my track record with panna cotta is not great - I once famously made a panna cotta with so much gelatin, you could literally bounce it off the counter. Luckily, this is not my recipe, so you can trust my dear mama on this. Enjoy!

2 tsp unflavored gelatin

1/4 cup black sesame powder

1 cup whole milk

1/4 cup sugar

1 cup heavy cream

1 Pour 1 cup of milk into a sauce pan and sprinkle in the gelatin. Mix and let it sit for 5 minutes.

2 Heat the milk with low heat until the gelatin dissolves, then turn off heat.

3 Add sugar into the pan, stir until dissolved.

4 Add heavy cream and sesame powder into the mixture. Stir well.

5 Let the mixture cool down to room temperature, then scoop into little jars or containers, cool in refrigerator for at least 4 hours or overnight. Serve cold.

PAPAYA MILK SMOOTHIE
木瓜牛奶 | Mùguā niúnǎi

Serving Size: 2

This beverage is popular in Taiwan and is a wonderful summertime treat. When we make this in the US, we usually add a bit of sugar to make it a yummy dessert drink. But in Taiwan, the papayas are huge and extremely sweet and don't need any sugar at all. Regardless, it's hard to go wrong with this drink!

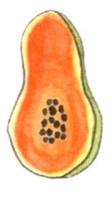

1/2 of a papaya

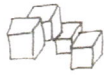

1 cup ice cubes

1/2 cup milk

Sugar, to taste

1 Cut a papaya in half and remove the seeds. Peel and cut into large chunks.

2 Add papaya, milk and ice in a blender. Blend until smooth.

3 Taste and add sugar as needed.

WHIPPED TARO SPREAD
芋泥 | Yù ní

Serving Size: 6

This spread is super easy to make and very convenient to have on hand as a yummy breakfast or dessert. I love putting this on toasted English muffins as a delightful breakfast. You can make this as pureed or as chunky as you like. I prefer a few taro chunks for texture - to do this, just mash the steamed taro lightly before making the spread.

1.5 cups steamed taro (see page 146)

1 cup heavy whipping cream

1 tbsp sugar

1 Pour heavy whipping cream and sugar into a stand mixer and beat on high for 5 minutes or until stiff peaks are formed.

2 Fold in steamed taro and use the mixing attachment to combine for another minute. Note: make sure the steamed taro is fully cooled before folding into cream.

3 Spread on toast or crackers or anything you like!

STEAMED BUNS

饅頭 | Mántou

Serving Size: 12 buns

While steamed buns are not necessarily super sweet in and of themselves, they are incredibly versatile and go well with sweet accompaniments. I treat these like English muffins - great with butter and jam or spreads but also delicious as part of a breakfast sandwich. We almost always have a batch of these in the freezer for a quick breakfast or on-the-go snack. Over the years, mom has also made various versions of this including brown sugar buns, purple rice buns, kabocha squash buns and more.

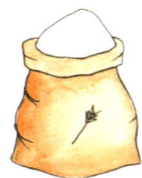

3-1/4 cup flour

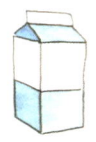

1-1/4 cup milk

1/4 cup sugar

1 tbsp cooking oil

2 tsp active dry yeast

1 Heat 1/2 the milk and mix in the sugar to dissolve it. Add in the remaining milk so that it becomes lukewarm.

2 Add yeast and let it sit for five minutes. It should be frothing a little at this point.

3 Combine milk and yeast mixture with oil and flour in a stand mixer and knead for 5 minutes.

4 Roll dough into a ball and cover with a damp towel. Prove in a warm place for one hour until it's doubled in size.

5 Using a kitchen scale, separate dough into 12 equally sized balls. This is where your elementary school math skills come into play!

6 Place each ball on a small piece of wax paper and place in a steamer, spaced out by 1-2 inches. Let it prove for 20 more minutes.

7 Bring water to a boil in the steamer and steam the buns for 9 minutes.

SWEET MUNG BEAN SOUP
綠豆湯 | Lǜdòu tāng

Serving Size: 6

Nothing screams Asian dessert as much as a sweet soup. This mung bean (or green bean) soup is usually served cold and is delightful on hot summer nights. The barley also provides a chewy texture akin to tapioca. We usually have a pot of this in the fridge during the peak of summer - so refreshing!

2/3 cup dried mung beans

1/3 cup barley

1/2 cup sugar

8 cups water

1 Rinse beans and barley with water, then drain.

2 Place beans and barley into a pressure cooker (like one whose name rhymes with Spinstant Spot) and add 5 cups of water.

3 Cook on "beans" setting and let it release pressure naturally when done.

4 While warm, add 1/2 cup sugar. Mix to dissolve sugar, then add 3 cups of cold water.

5 Cool on counter before placing in the refrigerator. Serve cold.

TWISTED PEANUT BUNS
花生麵包 | Huāshēng miànbāo

Serving Size: 12 buns

Mom always says she needs something sweet around the house at all times to have for breakfast or as a dessert after a meal. These peanut (and sometimes coconut) buns are the perfect sweet snack to have on hand and can usually be made with pantry ingredients.

1-1/2 cup peanut powder

1 stick butter, melted

1/2 cup granulated sugar

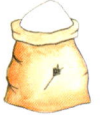

3-1/2 cups flour

2 tsp active dry yeast

300 mg milk

6 tbsp Greek yogurt

1/2 tsp salt

1 egg yolk

1 Heat up milk to make it lukewarm, then add active dry yeast and let it set for a few minutes.

2 Mix flour, yeast, milk, yogurt, salt and knead for 10 minutes. Cover the dough with a damp cloth and prove for an hour.

3 Make the filling by mixing the melted butter, powdered peanut and sugar.

4 Divide dough into two halves. Roll out each half into a 9x12 slab. Sprinkle the peanut filling over the entire slab, then fold into thirds longways.

5 With a rolling pin, flatten the folded dough a bit more to make the filling stick to the dough. The dough should be enveloping the filling. Cut the dough into 6 pieces.

6 Take each piece and cut 3-4 slits in it, longways. Then, stretch the dough while twisting it, tucking the ends in a loose knot. Prove for 30 minutes.

7 Brush with egg yolk, then bake for 15 minutes at 350 degrees until golden brown.

BLACK SESAME ROLLS
黑芝麻卷 | Hēi zhīma juǎn

Serving Size: 12 mini rolls
Like many Asian desserts, this one is not overly sweet. Black sesame lovers should rejoice as this recipe is filled with rich sesame paste and yields a beautiful swirl of flavor. You could also make this recipe with peanut powder + sugar or taro paste (see recipe on page 147).

3-1/4 cup flour

1 tbsp cooking oil

2 tsp active dry yeast

1-1/4 cup milk

1/4 & 1/3 cup sugar, separated

3/4 cup black sesame powder

1/3 cup butter, melted

1. Heat 3/4 cup of the milk in a small bowl and mix in 1/4 cup of sugar to dissolve it. Add in the remaining 1/2 cup of milk so that it becomes lukewarm.

2. Add yeast and let it sit for five minutes. It should be frothing a little at this point.

3. Combine the liquid mixture with oil and flour in a stand mixer and knead for 5 minutes.

4. Roll dough into a ball and cover with a damp towel. Prove in a warm place for one hour until it's doubled in size.

5. Make the black sesame filling by mixing the butter, sesame powder and sugar together into a paste.

6. Cut pieces of wax paper into 2-inch squares. Make 12 total - these will be used to prevent the rolls from sticking to the steamer basket.

7. Cut the dough in half and roll out each piece into a large flat rectangle (about 12x17). Spread black sesame filling over the dough, getting as close to the edges as possible.

8. Roll the dough up tightly along the long side so it's a long strand of rolled sesame paste and dough. Cut each strand into 6 pieces, dab with a bit of oil, and attach a small piece of wax paper.

9. Put the rolls in the steaming basket, place them in a warm spot, and prove for 20 minutes.

10. In the meantime, bring a pot of water to a boil. After second prove, place steamer baskets on the pot and steam for 10 minutes.

SWEET RED BEAN BUNS
豆沙包 | Dòushā bāo

Serving Size: 24 buns

If the beginnings of this recipe look familiar, it's because it uses the same steamed bread base as several other recipes (savory buns, black sesame rolls). This recipe is 'cheating' a bit because it uses a pre-made sweet red bean paste, but consider this a foundational recipe you can tweak with all sorts of fillings: homemade red bean paste, taro paste, or anything your heart desires.

3-1/4 cup flour

1-1/4 cup milk

2 tsp active dry yeast

1/4 & 1/4 cup sugar, separated

1 tbsp cooking oil

2 cans sweet red bean paste (16 oz each)

1 Heat 3/4 cup of the milk in a small bowl and mix in the sugar to dissolve it. Add in the remaining 1/2 cup of milk so that it becomes lukewarm.

2 Add yeast and let it sit for five minutes. It should be frothing a little at this point.

3 Combine milk and yeast mixture with oil and flour in a stand mixer and knead for 5 minutes.

4 Roll dough into a ball and cover with a damp towel. Prove in a warm place for one hour until it's doubled in size.

5 Cut pieces of wax paper into 2-inch squares. Make 24 total - these will be used to prevent the rolls from sticking to the steamer basket.

6 Divide the dough into 24 equal pieces using a kitchen scale. Roll out each piece of dough into a flat circle, about 4 inches wide. Make sure the edges of the dough are thinner and the center is thick.

7 Spoon 1 heaping tablespoon of red bean paste into the center of each dough circle. Then pinch and fold the bao, using the same method as the savory buns (see recipes).

8 Prove for 20 minutes in a warm place. While proving, bring a pot of water to a boil.

9 Steam buns for 10 minutes. Remove from heat and place on a cooling rack. Enjoy right away or freeze for later.

SWEET TARO SOUP
芋頭西米露 | Yùtou xī mǐ lù

Serving Size: 4

Our family loves soup, even when it comes to desserts. This is a comforting winter dessert, but I like to have it in the summer as well, even drinking it cold to the horror of my mother. It's super easy to make and the sweetness can be adjusted to your taste.

1 pound of taro

1/2 cup sugar

2 tbsp small tapioca pearls

Water, enough to cover the taro in a pot

1 can coconut milk (5.6 oz)

1 Cut the rind off of the taro and chop into small chunks.

2 Put the taro in a pot and add water until submerged. Boil water and cook taro until it is cooked through and soft (about 20 minutes).

3 Puree the mixture of taro and water with an immersion blender.

4 Add small tapioca and cook until tapioca is translucent (about 20 minutes).

5 Add coconut milk and bring to a boil. Add sugar, then remove from heat and serve warm.

SWEET RICE DUMPLINGS
甜粽子 | Tián zòngzi

Serving Size: 20

These small sweet rice dumplings make for a convenient dessert. Make a large batch at once and keep them in the freezer to heat up whenever you're craving a sweet treat.

40 bamboo leaves

8 rice cups of sticky rice (6 regular cups)

1 can of sweet red bean puree (16 oz)

20 Chinese red dates

2 cups peanuts

1/2 cup sugar

2 cups water

1. The night before: soak bamboo leaves in water with a heavy bowl to submerge and weigh it down. 40 leaves will make 20 rice dumplings.

2. Spread the red bean paste onto a square tray. Using a knife, score the red bean paste into 20 blocks. Place the tray in the freezer overnight to harden. This prevents the red bean paste from coating the rice later (which makes it harder to cook through).

3. Soak 6 cups (8 rice cups) of sticky rice in water for at least 6 hours.

4. Put the peanuts in an Instant Pot, cover with water and cook on 'beans' setting. Once done, let it release naturally, then add sugar and let it soak in the water.

5. After soaking the bamboo leaves, give each leaf a light scrub with a soft sponge, then dry with a clean towel.

6. Heat the peanuts with sugar water and rice on the stove top for 10 minutes. The rice will be partially, but not completely cooked.

7. Cook the dried Chinese red dates in water on the stove top for 10 minutes.

8. Prepare all the ingredients in separate bowls for easy assembly. Plan on the following amount for each dumpling: 1/3 cup sticky rice with peanuts, 1 block of red bean paste, 1 Chinese red date.

9. See the savory rice dumpling recipe for wrapping & steaming instructions .

THE LARDER

PICKLED MUSTARD GREENS
雪里红 | Xuě lǐ hóng

1. Wash 1 pound of mustard greens well. Let it soak in water for a bit to let all the dirt sink down, then drain.

2. Trim the roots off, then dice the mustard greens into pea-sized pieces.

3. Sprinkle with 2 tablespoons salt and massage into the greens using your hands.

4. Let the greens sit until it's ready - a minimum of 2-3 hours, overnight is best. After it's ready, use within a few days.

TIPS & TRICKS

- Buy the 'young' mustard greens that are smaller but better for pickling.

- Mustard greens should be prepared right away as they will start to yellow quickly. If they've already started to yellow, trim off any yellow leaves before starting.

- Enjoy as a topping on any soups, noodles or rice dishes for an extra bit of texture and salty goodness.

PICKLED LONG BEANS
泡豇豆 | Pào jiāngdòu

Growing up, there were all sorts of jars and containers in our fridge, many of which were reincarnated over and over again to hold new homemade delectables. Jam jars became dried scallop containers, salsa bottles re-purposed as fermented vegetable vessels, old spice jars contain new mystery ingredients. Pickled long beans is something my mom would make when the beans were in season and store in a former Prego jar. Once pickled, these long beans can be chopped up for ground pork dishes, dumplings, soup and more.

1 bunch long beans

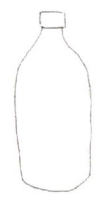

1-1/2 cup white vinegar

1/4 cup sugar

1/2 cup water

1 tsp salt

1 Wash long beans and fill a quart-sized mason jar, leaving an inch at the top to breathe.

2 In a separate bowl or small pitcher, combine white vinegar and water (3:1 ratio) along with sugar and salt. Mix to dissolve.

3 Pour liquid over long beans until it covers the top of the long beans

4 Refrigerate for 1 week before using. Keeps for 2 months in refrigerator.

MAMA JENG'S CHILI OIL
辣椒油 | Làjiāo yóu

Chili crisp is all the rage these days with so many artisan brands found in western markets and boutique stores. As a spice fanatic, I've pretty much tried them all, but truly nothing beats Mama Jeng's chili oil (also called chili crisp). It's flavorful enough to stand on it's own without needing other sauces, it's got a great blend of different chili peppers and it's just dang fun to make. It's hard not to ooh and ahh when the sizzling oil hits the peppers. Keep refrigerated and serve with anything that could use a little kick.

1/2 cup grape seed oil

2 tbsp crushed red pepper flakes

1 tbsp Szechuan peppercorns

2 tbsp cayenne pepper powder

1 Roast the Szechuan peppercorns in a saucepan until it just begins to smoke, then turn off and remove from heat.

2 Once cool, use a grinder to crush the peppercorns into a powder.

3 Mix all three peppers together in a heat resistant bowl.

4 Heat oil up in a small saucepan. When the oil starts to shimmer, spoon a few spoonfuls over the crushed peppers and let it sizzle. Follow with the remainder of the oil.

5 Pour into a jar for storage. Keep refrigerated.

SWEET STEAMED TARO

蒸芋頭 | Zhēng yùtou

Taro is a classic ingredient in many Chinese dishes. It grows wild in Taiwan's tropical climate and can be used in a variety of sweet and savory dishes. Mom seems to always have some steamed taro on hand to readily transform into a delicious dish. Some taro favorites include whipped taro spread, taro dessert soup, taro cake roll or savory taro cakes.

1 pound of taro

1/2 cup sugar

1 Slice the rough outer edges off of the taro. Cut the taro into small chunks.

2 Bring water to a boil in a steamer. Place taro chunks in a steamer-friendly bowl and steam for 30 minutes or until soft.

3 Mash taro with 1/2 cup sugar while warm.

4 Let cool, place in container and store in refrigerator for up to 3 days.

ABOUT THE AUTHOR

Nancy Jeng is the eldest (and clear favorite) daughter of the Jeng family. A native Californian (shout out Saratoga!) and adopted Texan (hook 'em Horns!), Nancy is equal parts amateur cook, serial hobbyist, and semi-professional marketer. With a spatula in one hand and paintbrush in another, you can usually find her doing too many things at once. Her unwitting taste-testers-slash-travel-companions include her mom, dad, sister Susan and husband Brett, all of whom have put up with more than they deserve. When she's not cooking, you can find her cuddling with Felix the pup or listening to the greatest songstress of all time, Mariah Carey.

www.ingramcontent.com/pod-product-compliance
Lightning Source LLC
Chambersburg PA
CBRC091211010526
44119CB00021B/375